For Courtney and Eddie. Bob and Carol. PJ and the

MW01489281

This book belongs to:

Mr. Flurry was getting ready for work, thinking his outfit would pass. Today he was going to start a new lesson with his Art class.

The media and materials were set, the best he could prepare. Mr. Flurry was confident he had everything square.

The students entered, eager to learn. Little did Mr. Flurry know how easily the tables might turn.

If all went according to plan this lesson would last just one week. Mr. Flurry was ready, about to speak.

But before the words could sputter out, a hand went up with a jerk. Before he could even be called, the student spouted, "How do giraffes work?"

Facing him now, a flood of hands. From question to question, countless demands.

There stood Mr. Flurry, now almost fully overwhelmed. Gone was the sense of control in the classroom he once helmed.

Clearly, they were running the show. Before he could muster a response, another hand went up, "So, did you, like, know Van Gogh?"

The bell rang before he could regain his composure. The students rushed out before anyone could get any closure.

BRRRRIIINNNNGGG

With the classroom empty, Mr. Flurry was in disbelief.

He was crushed.
Flabbergasted.
Completely Flummoxed.

While he stood, he tried to remember what mattered most: _Curiosity_. He decided then to tackle each inquiry with ferocity!

Before he knew it his board was full of facts and figures. Connecting questions and answers to dates and pictures.

The next morning the students entered without a peep. But Mr. Flurry was excited, even though he was lacking sleep.

The students sat and waited. Mr. Flurry was ready, and heavily caffeinated.

He bounced from point to picture.
Covering each topic with even mixture.

The students watched wide eyed, seeing this all unfold. Engaged and amused at all they were told.

There he stood, out of breath from the most intense of lessons. Then he asked, "So, any questions...?"

A hand went up, addressing the text.
Mr. Flurry was left profoundly perplexed.

He thought and thought, wishing he knew. "That's a great question. How about I find out, and get back to you?"

The bell rang out and the students left, forgetting the prior day's blunder. Instead, today they left excited and full of wonder.

As the classroom emptied, Mr. Flurry was content.

Wait... what's this hair he found, this random stray?
Could the last few days have started to turn him grey?

Made in United States
Orlando, FL
27 March 2025

59904852R00017